Celebrating You

(and the beautiful person you are)

Written by M.H. Clark · Design & Illustration by Jill Labieniec

Design & Creative Direction by Sarah Forster

This book is for you. For your kind heart, your dazzling spirit, your generosity, your laugh, your glow. It's a celebration of the person you are and the person you're working to become. Because you're beautiful, inside and out. Because you're worth celebrating.

You have a radiance
that's all your own.

You add extraordinary
to the everyday.

You have a kind and

pen heart.

You uplift others
around you.

Your spirit comes through ir

verything you do.

You make time for
the things that matter.

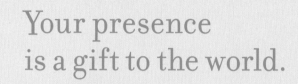

Your presence
is a gift to the world.

You're more than just
a little brilliant.
Sometimes, you glow.

You are strong.
Even when you
don't feel that way.

You're true to the best in others
and the best in yourself.

You know when to
create your own path.

You find adventure everywhere.

You set your mind
to something and
miracles happen.

Your bright future
is already on its way.

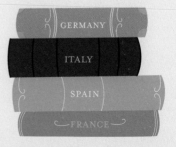

TRACK 10

TICKETS

You have a gift for
seeing possibility
in everything.

You make brave
changes for the better.

You celebrate
authenticity.

You listen to your heart,
and the world thanks you for it.

You have an inner
joy that spills out.

Your soul sparkles.

You throw open the
doors of opportunity.

You're a big part of what's good and right in the world.

You're loved for everything you are and all that you're becoming.

You bloom with
courage and grace.

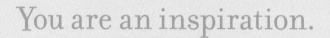

You are an inspiration.

You are beautiful.

COMPENDIUM®

live inspired

With special thanks to the
entire Compendium family.

Credits:
Written by: M.H. Clark
Design & Illustration by: Jill Labieniec
Design & Creative Direction by: Sarah Forster
Edited by: Jennifer Pletsch

ISBN: 978-1-932319-99-6

12th printing. Printed in China with soy inks.